Piano • Vocal

KURT WEILL
FROM BERLIN TO BROADWAY

The songs of KURT WEILL
In collaboration with

—

Maxwell Anderson
Marc Blitzstein
Bertolt Brecht
Michael Feingold
Ira Gershwin
Paul Green
Langston Hughes
Alan Jay Lerner
Ogden Nash

—

**HAL LEONARD
PUBLISHING
CORPORATION**

Home Office: National Sales Office:
960 East Mark Street   8112 West Bluemound Road
Winona MN 55987   Milwaukee WI 53213

Kurt Weill, circa 1920

FROM BERLIN TO BROADWAY

Editorial Consultant: Judy Bell/The Richmond Organization
All photos courtesy of the Kurt Weill Foundation for Music

4

Weill at Brook House. New York City, N.Y.
1940's

"Mack The Knife" has previously been a hit for LOUIS ARMSTRONG (1956 & 1959), the DICK HYMAN TRIO (1956), BOBBY DARIN (1959 & 1979), and ELLA FITZGERALD (1960). In America it has been even more popular, being the only song to become a hit on eight separate occasions.

Record Mirror, London, England
May 5, 1984

The unique melody of "Mack The Knife" first electrified the world in 1928, when Kurt Weill and Bertolt Brecht's **The Threepenny Opera** was given its world premiere in Berlin. Their bold adaptation of the 200 year-old **Beggars' Opera** was the theatrical sensation of the Twenties. The Berlin production was followed by innumerable performances all over the European continent, the work having been translated into 18 different languages. Kurt Weill, the composer of the work's provocative and totally unorthodox musical score, was only twenty-eight years old at the time.

Born on March 2, 1900, the son of a cantor in Dessau, Germany, Kurt Weill's musical gifts became apparent at a very early age. Shunning the usual children's games, he earned the family nickname of "attic composer," when he chose to disappear into the attic to compose music instead of joining the fun. Although his parents would have clearly preferred for young Kurt to become a doctor or a businessman, they supported his studies of piano, counterpoint and harmony - at first under Albert Bind (the leading conductor of Dessau's opera house) and later at the Berlin College of Music under Engelbert Humperdinck, the composer of the opera **Hänsel und Gretel**.

Already at the age of 19, young Weill accepted the position of conductor at the small opera house in Luedenscheid. But after only one year of serving in this capacity, he decided that composing, not conducting, was more to his liking. Once more he returned to Berlin in order to join the master classes of the famous pianist-composer Ferruccio Busoni, under whose guidance and considerable influence he wrote his First Symphony, various orchestral and vocal works, as well as chamber music. His first major breakthrough as a composer came with the performance of his String Quartet, op. 8, at the distinguished Baden-Baden Music Festival in 1922. Not only did this performance bring him considerable critical acclaim, but also a long-term contract with one of Europe's most prominent publishing houses, Universal Edition in Vienna.

Various other works followed with equal success, and by the time Weill's first opera, **The Protagonist**, was produced at Dresden's opera house, the composer had established himself as one of the leading figures of modern music in Central Europe.

Following the trend of the times, Weill had pursued atonal techniques and the style of "free dissonance" in his musical language. His collaboration with the playwright and poet Bertolt Brecht brought him to the realization that such music was beyond the understanding of a wide public. In their first collaborative effort, the **Little Mahagonny** (1927) later to be developed into the full-length opera, **The Rise And Fall Of The City Of Mahagonny**), Weill introduced the "Alabama Song," wherein he pared down his musical vocabulary to the most basic chords and progressions to a melody as haunting as any popular and "hummable" tune could be — but with an edge to the sound that no sentimentality could assimilate.

*Weill (far left), Lenya with sign "für Weill" (stage right), Brecht (far right): 1927, Baden-Baden — **Mahagonny Songspiel**.*

*Lenya in the 1954 New York production of **Threepenny Opera**.*

*Lenya, Harald Paulsen in **Aufstieg und Fall der Stadt Mahagonny** (Berlin, 1930).*

*Walter Huston, Jeanne Madden in **Knickerbocker Holiday** (New York, 1938).*

Lenya and Weill, 1929

With the phenomenal success of the next Weill-Brecht collaboration, **The Threepenny Opera** (1928), Weill's melodies had indeed been able to reach the widest audience possible, since now every radio station, record and music shop was breaking into a consumer industry.

Among the ensuing Weill-Brecht collaborations, **Happy End** (1929), was the least successful at the time, but is presently experiencing a popularity that almost equals that of **The Threepenny Opera**, with "Surabaya Johnny" and "Bilbao Song" as special favorites.

While dark political clouds were gathering over Germany, Weill wrote the opera **The Pledge** and the musical play **The Silverlake** (1933), the latter containing a ballad aimed directly at the dictator Adolf Hitler. Weill was blacklisted by the Nazis and had to leave Germany overnight.

A commission to write his Second Symphony brought Weill to Paris, where he spent his first two years in exile. In the fall of 1935, Weill and his wife Lotte Lenya (whom he had married in 1926 and who was to become the most memorable interpreter of his songs) moved to New York on an invitation to write the music for a biblical spectacle, **The Eternal Road**. Deeply impressed by the Gershwins' **Porgy And Bess,** which was then running at the Alvin Theatre in New York, Weill decided with characteristic assurance that Broadway was to be the American musical theatre scene with which he wanted to be involved.

While the opening of **The Eternal Road** had to be postponed because of financial difficulties, Weill accepted an offer by the Group Theatre to write the score for an anti-war play, **Johnny Johnson**, by the Pulitzer prize-winner Paul Green. **Johnny Johnson** opened in November 1936 and totally startled both audiences and critics by its boldly innovative concept of interpolating story line with music, as for example, an entire ballet sequence advancing the plot as an integrated part of the whole (an innovation in the world of musical comedy usually attributed to the much later **Oklahoma!** by Rodgers and Hammerstein). In addition, Weill did something unheard of on Broadway since the days of Victor Herbert: he insisted on doing his own orchestrations, a practice he never abandoned.

Although **Johnny Johnson** was not a commercial success, it established Weill as a theatre composer of importance. (The lyricist Lorenz Hart is supposed to have said to Weill after hearing **Johnny Johnson**: "What are you trying to do: put people like me out of business?")

Weill's next Broadway project **Knickerbocker Holiday** (1938) was written in collaboration with playwright Maxwell Anderson, who was to become one of Weill's closest personal friends. **Knickerbocker Holiday** concerns itself with the evils of dictatorship and the value of freedom. To express their convictions, the authors drew modern parallels by telling the story of the tyrannical Governor Pieter Stuyvesant, who had attempted to suppress the liberties of the people of New Amsterdam in the early 1800's. In a bold piece of casting, Weill suggested the celebrated actor Walter Huston, who had never before sung a note in a legitimate theatre, for the part of Stuyvesant — setting an example for the much later casting of Rex Harrison as Professor Higgins in **My Fair Lady**. It was for the non-singer Walter Huston that one of Weill's most beloved melodies, "September Song" was written. But despite Huston's memorable interpretation, "September Song" became a "hit" only after Bing Crosby recorded it some time later.

Weill and Anderson continued their collaboration with a dramatic cantata, **The Ballad of the Magna Carta** for Burgess Meredith (who had introduced them to each other), which had its first performance in 1940 over CBS Radio, with Meredith as the narrator.

Ceremonies celebrating the display of the Magna Carta, Washington, D.C. (1976) with Mike Mansfield, Carl Albert, Tip O'Neill. The Anderson-Weill cantata "Ballad of Magna Carta" was performed.

Weill's next musical, **Lady In The Dark,** with a book by Moss Hart and lyrics by Ira Gershwin, was his first big commercial success in America. **Lady** tells the story of one Liza Elliott, chief editor of a famous fashion magazine, who cannot make up her mind about anything and consequently seeks the help of a psychiatrist. In the form of several dream sequences — each one a musical entity in itself — the analysis reveals Liza's schizophrenic personality, with "The Saga Of Jenny" (the lady who can't make up her mind) revealing most eloquently Liza's dilemma in a most sophisticated, hilarious fashion.

*Gertrude Lawrence with chorus, "The Saga of Jenny" from **Lady in the Dark** (New York, 1941).*

Just a couple of years later, Weill had another "hit" on his hands when **One Touch Of Venus** (1943), with a book by S.J. Perelman and lyrics by Ogden Nash, opened to rave reviews. It is the story of a young barber who sees a statue of the goddess Venus in a museum and — just for fun — slips his engagement ring on the statue's finger. This brings the marble goddess back to life in the Twentieth Century, which totally bewilders her, and after a series of adventures, she finally turns into a marble statue again. Although **One Touch Of Venus** made no larger pretense than the wish to entertain, this new treatment of the classical Galatea theme presented wit and elegance at their very best — elements that also distinguished Weill's next effort, **The Firebrand of Florence.**

With a book by Edwin Justus Meyer and lyrics by Ira Gershwin — based on an episode in the life of the Italian sculptor Benvenuto Cellini — this **Firebrand** was nothing less than a comic opera with ariettas, recitatives and concerted ensembles written for operatic voices. Misdirected and badly cast, **The Firebrand** did not have any success at all.

*The Company of **The Firebrand of Florence** (New York, 1945).*

But this failure did not stop Weill from pursuing his dream of an "American Opera," a dream he was able to realize in 1947, when his **Street Scene** — a book by Elmer Rice and lyrics by Langston Hughes — opened on Broadway. ("The most important step toward significant American opera yet encountered in the musical theatre." - **New York Times**). The opera deals with everyday life in the ghettos of New York's lower East Side. The main plot centers on the Maurrant family: the embittered husband Frank; his unhappy wife Anna, who carries on an illicit love affair with the milkman; and their daughter Rose, whose romance with a Jewish law student never has a real chance. A colorful cast of characters — an Italian music teacher, gossiping neighbors of different ethnic origins, peddlers, children and street vendors - present a symphony of the big city with all of its daily problems: love, longing, disappointment, prejudice and violence as well.

*Randolph Symonette as Mr. Maurrant in **Street Scene** (Düsseldorf, 1955).*

The success of **Street Scene** encouraged Weill to turn once more to a form of theatre he had created during his collaboration with Brecht: the "school opera" — opera written for schools — to be performed by and for students. Working with Arnold Sundgaard, Weill dramatized the old folk song "Down In The Valley" — the tragic tale of Jenny and Brack, young lovers who enjoy but a brief moment of happiness before a cruel act of injustice puts a violent end to the young man's life. Far away from Broadway this time, **Down In The Valley** was first performed at Indiana University, Bloomington, Indiana, in 1947. It has since become one of the most popular and frequently performed "school operas" and has been televised several times in this country, Great Britain and Germany.

Hardly ever affording himself a rest (in between his Broadway work, Weill wrote several important scores for Hollywood as well), Weill's next Broadway musical was once more a total departure from accustomed forms. In collaboration with Alan Jay Lerner, he wrote **Love Life** which tells the story of the disintegration of a marriage in the United States — from colonial days up to the present — in a series of sketches and vaudeville acts. The musical had a respectable run of over 200 performances, but a recording strike at the time prevented the music from being recorded and finding a wider audience.

Maxwell Anderson, Lenya, Weill (1940's).

In 1949, Weill once more collaborated with Maxwell Anderson when they adapted Alan Paton's moving novel **Cry, The Beloved Country** for the music stage under the title **Lost In The Stars**. The story takes place in South Africa and centers on two fathers: the simple and very poor black minister Stephen Kumalo and the wealthy, white plantation owner James Jarvis. Stephen's son Absalom has disappeared in the slums of Johannesburg, where James' son Arthur is devoting his energy to social work for the betterment of the black community. By a cruel twist of fate, it is Absalom who accidentally shoots Arthur during a holdup. When the case comes to trial, Absalom's confederates lie about their presence at the crime and get off scot-free, while Absalom — on his father's advice — speaks the truth, fully aware of the consequence: death by hanging. Deeply moved by the moral courage of both Stephen and Absalom, James Jarvis extends his hand in friendship to Stephen, as both men sit together, watching the hours tick by on the morning of Absalom's death.

Lenya and Weill with Wooly at
Brook House, New City, NY (1940's)

While **Lost In The Stars** was still running on Broadway, Weill was felled by a heart attack and died on April 3, 1950, leaving only sketches for his next project: a folk opera based on Mark Twain's **Huckleberry Finn.**

Weill was indeed fortunate enough to experience outstanding success during his lifetime. However, the tremendous impact his work has had on the world's musical theatre — and in particular on the American musical theatre — only now is coming into focus. Inasmuch as America does not yet have the kind of musical repertory theatre which could present revivals of the great classics of the American Musical (without having to depend on costly and risky commercial revivals on Broadway), a great many of Weill's musicals are as yet unknown to the younger generations.

Therefore, the present song book, highlighting Weill's most endearing and enduring melodies, serves a truly important function in acquainting a new generation — and at the same time, reacquainting an older one — with the music of one of the Twentieth Century's great masters.

LYS SYMONETTE
Faculty of the Curtis Institute of Music
Philadelphia, PA

Mack The Knife
(From "THE THREEPENNY OPERA")

English Words by MARC BLITZSTEIN
Original German Words by BERT BRECHT
Music by KURT WEILL

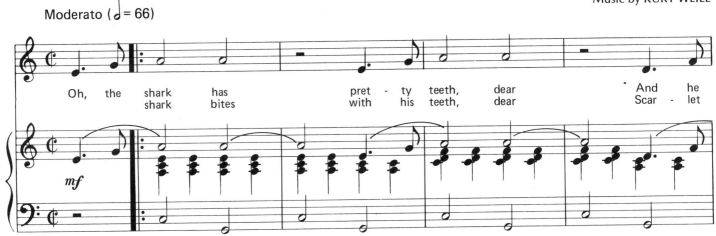

Lou - ie Mil - ler dis - ap - peared, dear Af - ter

draw - ing out his cash. And Mac - heath spends

like a sail - or Did our boy do some - thing

rash? Su - key Taw - dry, Jen - ny Div - er,

p

mf

The Bilbao Song
(From "HAPPY END")

English Words by MICHAEL FEINGOLD
Original German Words by BERT BRECHT
Music by KURT WEILL

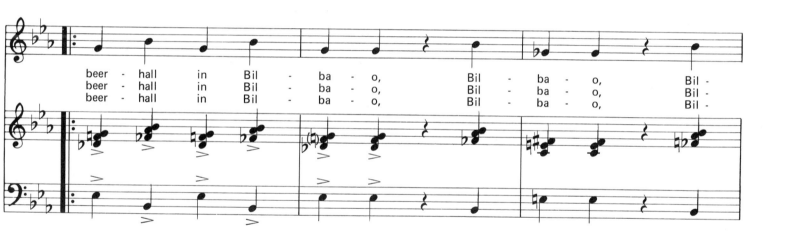

19

Surabaya Johnny
(From "HAPPY END")

English Words by MICHAEL FEINGOLD
Original German Words by BERT BRECHT
Music by KURT WEILL

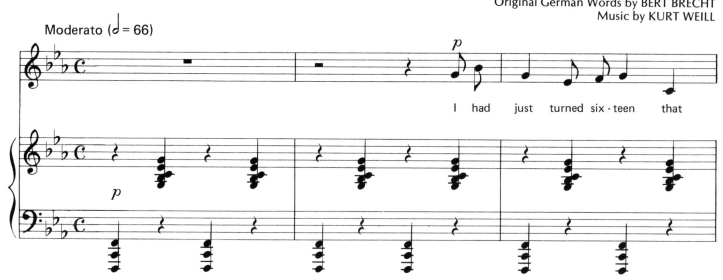

I had just turned six - teen that

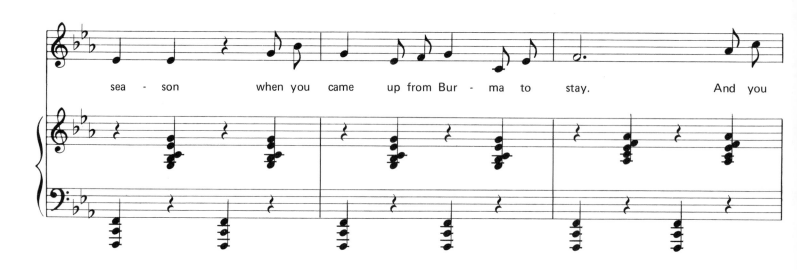

sea - son when you came up from Bur - ma to stay. And you

told me I ought to trav - el with you, You were sure it would be o -

kay. When I asked how you earned your liv - ing I can

still hear what you said to me: You had some kind of job with the

rail - way, and had noth - ing to do with the sea. You said a

lot, John - ny, all one big lie, John - ny. You cheat-ed me blind, John - ny, from the min-ute we

why'm I feel - ing so blue? You have no heart, John-ny,

and I still love you so! At the start ev' -ry day was

Sun - day, till we went on our way one fine night. And be - fore two more weeks were_

o - ver you thought noth - ing I did was right. So we trekked up and down through the

26

Pun - jab from the source of the riv - er to the sea: When I look at my face in the

mir - ror there's an old wo - man star - ing back at me. You did-n't want

love, John-ny, you want - ed cash, John-ny, but I saw your lips, John-ny, and that was

that. You want-ed it all, John-ny, I gave you more, John-ny. *(spoken)* *Take that damn*

pipe out of your mouth, you rat! Su - ra - ba - ya John - ny, no one's

mean - er than you. Su - ra - ba - ya John - ny, (spoken) my God, and

I still love you so! Su - ra - ba - ya John - ny, why'm I

feel - ing so blue? You have no heart, John - ny, and I still love you

so! I would nev - er have thought of ask - ing where you got that pec - u - liar__ name, but from one end of the coast to the oth - er you were known ev'-ry-where we came. And one day in a two - bit flop house I'll wake up to the roar of the sea, and you'll leave with-out one word of warn - ing on the

ship wait-ing down at the quay.* You have no heart, John-ny, you're just a

louse, John-ny. How can you go, John-ny, and leave me flat? You're still my

love, John - ny, like the day we met, John - ny. *(spoken)* Take that damn

pipe out of your mouth, you rat! Su - ra - ba - ya John - ny,

*pronounced "key"

There's Nowhere To Go But Up
(From the Musical Play "KNICKERBOCKER HOLIDAY")

Lyrics by MAXWELL ANDERSON
Music by KURT WEILL

The bird flies east,   The bird flies west,
Up one street,   And down one street,

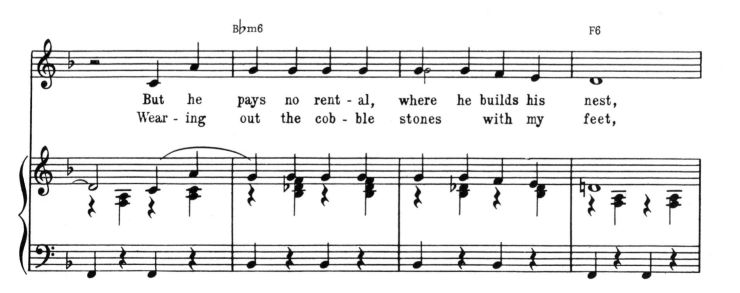

But he pays no rent - al, where he builds his nest,
Wear - ing out the cob - ble stones with my feet,

It Never Was You
(From the Musical Play "KNICKERBOCKER HOLIDAY")

Words by MAXWELL ANDERSON
Music by KURT WEILL

September Song

(From the Musical Play "KNICKERBOCKER HOLIDAY")

Lyrics by MAXWELL ANDERSON
Music by KURT WEILL

plied her with tears in the lieu of pearls And as
lit - tle to of - fer but the songs they sing And a

time came a - round she came my way, As time came a - round she came.
plen - ti - ful waste of time of day, A plen - ti - ful waste of time.

Refrain *(with expression)*

Oh, it's a long, long while From May to De - cem - ber, ___

But the days grow short, ___ When you reach Sep -

43

Alabama Song
(From "THE RISE AND FALL OF THE CITY OF MAHAGONNY")

Written by BERT BRECHT
and KURT WEILL

Moderato assai (♩= 69)

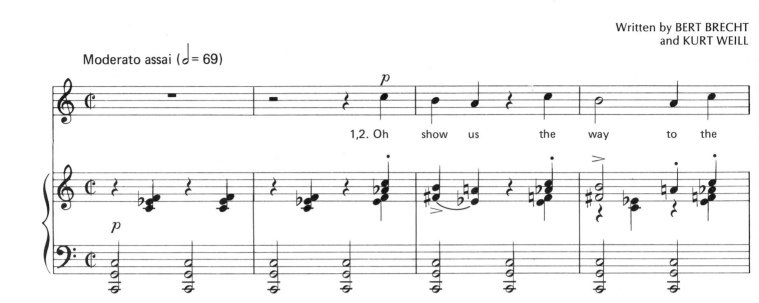

we don't find the next {whis-ky bar, / lit-tle dol-lar,} I tell you we must die! I

tell you we must die! I tell you, I tell you, I tell you we must

die! Oh! Moon _____

_____ of A - la - ba - ma we now _____

Listen To My Song (Johnny's Song)

(From the Musical Production "JOHNNY JOHNSON")

Lyrics by PAUL GREEN
Music by KURT WEILL

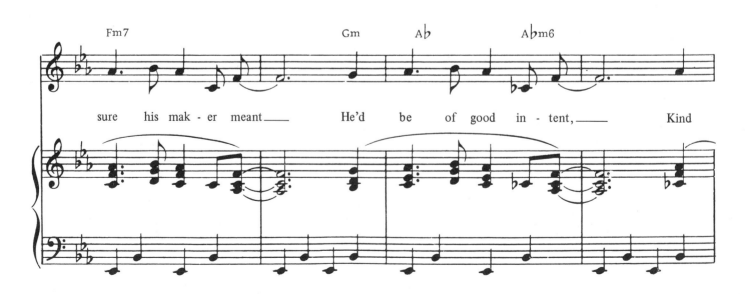

Mon Ami, My Friend
(From the Musical Production "JOHNNY JOHNSON")

Lyrics by PAUL GREEN
Music by KURT WEILL

Speak Low
(From the Musical Production "ONE TOUCH OF VENUS")

Lyrics by OGDEN NASH
Music by KURT WEILL

Sing Me Not A Ballad

(From the Musical Production "THE FIREBRAND OF FLORENCE")

Lyrics by IRA GERSHWIN
Music by KURT WEILL

The Saga Of Jenny
(From the Musical Production "LADY IN THE DARK")

Lyrics by IRA GERSHWIN
Music by KURT WEILL

This Is New
(From the Musical Production "LADY IN THE DARK")

Lyrics by IRA GERSHWIN
Music by KURT WEILL

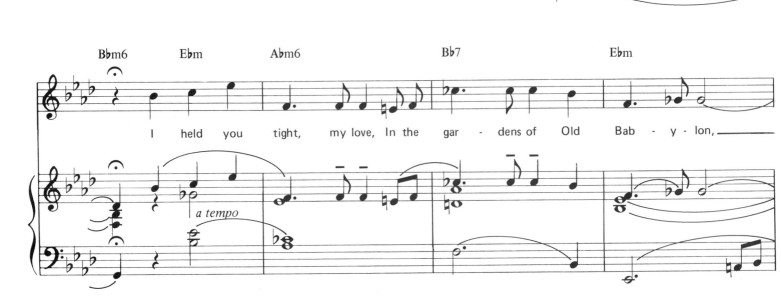

With you I used to roam through the Pleas - ure Dome of Kub - la Kahn,

I held you tight, my love, In the gar - dens of Old Bab - y - lon,

My Ship
(From the Musical Production "LADY IN THE DARK")

Lyrics by IRA GERSHWIN
Music by KURT WEILL

What Good Would The Moon Be?

(From the Musical Production "STREET SCENE")

Lyrics by LANGSTON HUGHES
Music by KURT WEILL

I've looked in the win - dows at dia - monds, They're beau - ti - ful, but they're cold. I've seen Broad-way stars in fur coats that cost a

A Boy Like You
(From the Musical Production "STREET SCENE")

Lyrics by LANGSTON HUGHES
Music by KURT WEILL

crowd. Such a man-ly arm I'll have to lean on

When I walk down the A - ve - nue.

Some-bod-y will al-ways be my stand-by, Who do you think it is? Guess

who? Some-bod-y I know will al - ways

love me ____ Read - y with a help - ing

hand. Some-bod - y will nev - er, no, not ev - er for -

get to care and un - der - stand. Yes, that is the grand - est

feel - ing, That an - y wo-man ev - er knew,

To know I have some-bod-y won-der-ful, To

know I have a boy like you.

To

know I have a boy like you!

The Little Gray House
(From the Musical Production "LOST IN THE STARS")

Words by MAXWELL ANDERSON
Music by KURT WEILL

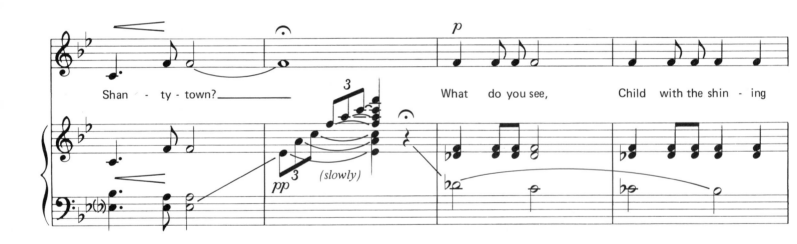

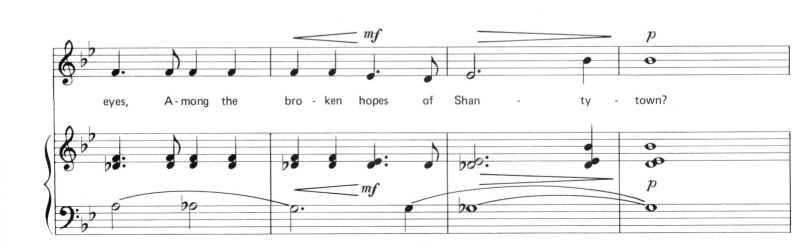

wat - er from the bot - tom of the hill.
kitch - en to bake to - mor - row's bread.
And the white Star of
And she al - ways has

To Coda

Beth - le - hem _____ grows in the yard, _____
love e - nough _____ to take you in. _____
And I can't

real - ly des - cribe it, but I'm try - ing hard. _____ It's not much to

tell a - bout, _____ It's not much to pic - ture out, _____ And the on - ly thing

dolce espr.

Lost In The Stars
(From the Musical Production "LOST IN THE STARS")

Lyrics by MAXWELL ANDERSON
Music by KURT WEILL

Stay Well
(From the Musical Production "LOST IN THE STARS")

Lyrics by MAXWELL ANDERSON
Music by KURT WEILL

Trouble Man
(From the Musical Production "LOST IN THE STARS")

Lyrics by MAXWELL ANDERSON
Music by KURT WEILL

Assai moderato *(ben ritmato)*
Refrain

Trou - ble man, trou - ble man since you've been gone,_____ Some - how I

man - age liv - ing here a - lone. All day long you don't catch me

weep - ing, But oh, God, help me when it comes time for sleep - ing, When it comes

time for sleep - ing here a - lone._____

Here I'll Stay
(From the Musical Production "LOVE LIFE")

Lyrics by ALAN JAY LERNER
Music by KURT WEILL

Love Song

(From the Musical Production "LOVE LIFE")

Lyrics by ALAN JAY LERNER
Music by KURT WEILL

green to dol - lar bills. Yes, I've heard 'em all, Mis - ter, But I

can't go sing 'em back, I sing an - oth - er song a - long the track.

Refrain *(con molto espressione)*

I sing a song a - bout the o - cean, _____

Sing of how end - less is the o - cean, _____

Susan's Dream
(From the Musical Production "LOVE LIFE")

Lyrics by ALAN JAY LERNER
Music by KURT WEILL

119

Green-Up Time

(From the Musical Production "LOVE LIFE")

Lyrics by ALAN JAY LERNER
Music by KURT WEILL